W9-DFM-206

0 00 30 0290480 7

HAYNER PUBLIC LIBRARY DISTRICT
ALTON, ILLINOIS

OVERDUES .10 PER DAY. MAXIMUM FINE
COST OF BOOKS. LOST OR DAMAGED BOOKS
ADDITIONAL $5.00 SERVICE CHARGE.

The Really **Wild Life** of **Birds** of **Prey**™

VULTURES

DOUG WECHSLER

The Rosen Publishing Group's
PowerKids Press™
New York

HAYNER PUBLIC LIBRARY DISTRICT
ALTON, ILLINOIS

For Frank Gill, ornithologist extraordinaire, worthy ex-boss, and expert in the ways of the vulture.

Thanks to Uncle Eddie for the bad vulture joke.

About the Author
Wildlife biologist, ornithologist, and photographer Doug Wechsler has studied birds, snakes, frogs, and other wildlife around the world. Doug Wechsler works at The Academy of Natural Sciences of Philadelphia, a natural history museum. As part of his job, he travels to rain forests and remote parts of the world to take pictures of birds. He has taken part in expeditions to Ecuador, the Philippines, Borneo, Cuba, Cameroon, and many other countries.

Published in 2001 by The Rosen Publishing Group, Inc.
29 East 21st Street, New York, NY 10010

Copyright © 2001 by The Rosen Publishing Group, Inc.

All rights reserved. No part of this book may be reproduced in any form without permission in writing from the publisher, except by a reviewer.

First Edition

Book Design: Michael de Guzman

Photo Credits: p. 4 © B. K. Wheeler/VIREO; p. 7 © A. Morris/VIREO and © Rob Curtis/VIREO; p. 8 © A. & E. Morris/VIREO; p. 11 © R. Day/VIREO; p. 12 © A. Morris/VIREO; pp. 15, 16 © N. G. Smith/VIREO; p. 19 © J. R. Woodward/VIREO; p. 20 © R. & S. Day/VIREO; p. 22 © Rob Curtis/VIREO. All photographs from VIREO (Visual Resources for Ornithology), The Academy of Natural Sciences' worldwide collection of bird photographs.

Wechsler, Doug.
    Vultures / by Doug Wechsler.—1st ed.
      p. cm.—(Really wild life of birds of prey)
    Summary: Describes the physical characteristics, behavior, and habitat of this large scavenger bird.
    ISBN 0-8239-5594-X (alk. paper)
    1. Vultures—Juvenile literature. [1.Vultures.] I. Title.

    QL696.F32 W426 2000
    598.9'2—dc21   00-024768

Manufactured in the United States of America

J5989
WEC

AEA-7750

CONTENTS

SCAVENGERS OF THE BIRD WORLD

Vultures are large birds of **prey**. They have ugly, bare heads with no feathers. Vultures are **scavengers**. Three kinds of vultures live in North America. The largest of the three, the California condors, are among the biggest flying birds. They are about 9 feet (2.7 m) across from wing tip to wing tip. Turkey vultures have a good sense of smell. Their **wingspan** can be 6 1/2 feet (1.9 m) long. Black vultures are the smallest of the vultures, but they are still large as birds go. Their wingspan is about 5 feet (1.5 m) long. Four more **species** can be found in South America. Vultures also live in Africa, Asia, and Europe. These vultures are not closely related to the vultures of North and South America.

Vultures are mostly blackish in color. Their heads look small because they have no feathers.

DEAD DINNERS

Vultures eat **carrion**. Carrion is dead animal meat. Dead cows, dead fish, and dead turtles are nice meals for a vulture. Vultures would rather eat fresh carrion, but they usually have to eat carrion rotten. This is because it is easier to find a dead animal after it starts to smell. It can also be hard for vultures to tear apart a freshly killed animal. They wait for the dead animal to **decay** and break open.

Turkey vultures feed on carrion. They often eat in groups. They will eat almost any kind of dead animal.

DOUG SAYS
WHAT DID ONE
VULTURE SAY TO
ANOTHER?
CARRY ON, SAM.

FAST OR FEAST

Dead animals can be hard to find. Vultures can go for long periods of time without eating. A turkey vulture can easily last for two weeks without having a meal. A California condor can **fast** for a much longer time. When it does find a big meal, a vulture will stuff itself until its **crop** bulges. The crop is a sac where food is stored before it goes into the stomach. On California condors, the skin outside the crop is bright pink. The pink bulge tells the world that the condor has had a big dinner.

Vultures have very strong, sharp beaks.

VULTURE VOMIT

Thinking about what vultures eat is enough to make you want to throw up. Vultures do not just think about it. They do vomit for many reasons. Vultures feed their young by **regurgitating** carrion. When the **nestlings** are very small, the parents regurgitate partly **digested** meat for them. When the nestlings get larger, the parents cough up undigested meat.

If you are lucky enough to find a vulture nest, beware! The birds will defend themselves by vomiting. That is something your mom or dad may not enjoy washing off your clothes. Sometimes vultures are so stuffed with food they can hardly fly. If an enemy comes near, a vulture may throw up its meal so that it is light enough to fly away.

Vultures feed their young by regurgitating carrion for them.

THE BEST SMELLING VULTURE

Only a few kinds of birds have a good sense of smell. The turkey vulture is one of these birds. Even while flying above a forest, turkey vultures can smell food hidden on the ground below. Turkey vultures are best at finding carrion when it has been dead for at least one day.

Gas pipeline companies put a chemical in natural gas that smells a little like carrion. When a gas pipe leaks, the vultures start to circle the area around the leak. By doing this, the circling vultures show the repair people where to look for leaks.

Turkey vultures have a good sense of smell. It is easier for them to locate carrion if it has been dead for at least a day.

VULTURE FOLLOWS VULTURE

All vultures pay attention to other vultures. They will follow one another to a source of food. Unlike turkey vultures, black vultures do not have a good sense of smell. They do have great eyesight, though. Black vultures fly high watching for other vultures. When a black vulture sees a turkey vulture fly down into the forest, it follows. Black vultures are smaller than turkey vultures, but they are still very **aggressive**. A black vulture will steal a good meal from a turkey vulture and leave only the scraps.

Black vultures are forceful when it comes to meals. They will steal food from turkey vultures and leave only small pieces.

DOUG SAYS
VULTURES ARE THE BIRDS MOST LIKELY TO CAUSE AIRPLANE ACCIDENTS BECAUSE THEY ARE BIG AND THEY FLY HIGH.

CHEAP FLIGHTS

Vultures do everything they can to save energy. They flap their wings as little as possible. They rely on their huge wings to glide through the air. They search for **thermals**, warm air rising from the ground. When they find a thermal, the vultures circle upward letting the rising air carry them. Then they glide slowly downward until they find another thermal. Vultures also ride the breezes that sweep up the sides of hills and mountains.

A black vulture glides through the air. Vultures like to save their energy by flapping their wings as little as possible!

MIGRATION

Frozen **carcasses** are hard to eat. Turkey vultures that spend the summer in southern Canada and the northern United States **migrate** south for the winter. They migrate because food is harder to find in the winter. Many turkey vultures from west of the Rocky Mountains migrate all the way to Central and South America. Each fall more than one million turkey vultures are seen migrating along the Caribbean coast of Mexico. In the winter, these turkey vultures hunt in grasslands, tropical forests, and farms in Central and South America.

Turkey vultures migrate south for the winter. Food is hard to find where snow is deep.

DOUG SAYS
VULTURES HAVE
BEEN AROUND
FOR MORE THAN
35 MILLION
YEARS.

YOU CALL THAT A NEST?

Vultures do not waste energy building a nest. Instead they lay their eggs right on the ground. They find out-of-the-way places to call home. A small cave on a cliff, a space between large boulders in the woods, a hole in a fallen tree, or an empty building away from people all make good nest sites. Vultures move to and from the nest very carefully. They try not to let their enemies see them.

Vultures lay two eggs, usually right on the ground.

THE CLEANUP CREW

Vultures provide a great service to us and other animals. They find dead animals and clean them up. A rotten carcass is full of disease-causing germs. If the germs wash into the water, they can make animals sick. The germs usually do not harm the vulture. Next time you see a vulture soaring high in the sky, say, "Thank you for keeping this place clean."

GLOSSARY

aggressive (uh-GREH-siv) Taking the first step in an attack.

carcasses (CAR-cus-sez) Bodies of dead animals.

carrion (KAHR-ee-un) Dead, rotting flesh of animals.

crop (KROP) A sac inside the neck of many birds where food is stored.

decay (dee-KAY) To rot.

digested (dy-JEST-ed) When your body has broken down the food you eat for energy.

fast (FAST) To go without food.

migrate (MY-grayt) When large groups of birds, animals, or people move from one place to another.

nestlings (NEST-lingz) Young birds that are still living in the nest.

prey (PRAY) An animal that is eaten by another animal for food.

regurgitating (re-GER-juh-tayt-ing) Vomiting, or throwing up, partly digested food.

scavengers (SCAV-en-jerz) Animals that feed on dead animals.

species (SPEE-sheez) A single kind of plant or animal. For example, all people are one species.

thermals (THER-mulz) Warm air rising from the ground. Often thermals rise from places where the sun heats the earth the most, like plowed fields or parking lots.

wingspan (WING-span) The distance from wing tip to wing tip when a bird's wings are stretched out.

INDEX

WEB SITES

To learn more about vultures, check out these Web sites:

http://www.raptor.cvm.umn.edu
http://www.id/blm.gov/pobnca/index.html
http://www.acnatsci.org/vireo (Readers can order a raptor slide set.)